EXPLORE THE U.S.A.

NEW YORK

Cindy Rodriguez

Go to **www.av2books.com**, and enter this book's unique code.

BOOK CODE

V893508

AV² by Weigl brings you media enhanced books that support active learning.

AV² provides enriched content that supplements and complements this book. Weigl's AV² books strive to create inspired learning and engage young minds in a total learning experience.

Your AV² Media Enhanced books come alive with...

 Audio
Listen to sections of the book read aloud.

 **Video**
Watch informative video clips.

 Embedded Weblinks
Gain additional information for research.

 Try This!
Complete activities and hands-on experiments.

 Key Words
Study vocabulary, and complete a matching word activity.

 Quizzes
Test your knowledge.

 Slide Show
View images and captions, and prepare a presentation.

... and much, much more!

Published by AV² by Weigl
350 5ᵗʰ Avenue, 59ᵗʰ Floor
New York, NY 10118
Website: www.av2books.com   www.weigl.com

Library of Congress Cataloging-in-Publication Data
Rodriguez, Cindy.
 New York / Cindy Rodriguez.
    p. cm. -- (Explore the U.S.A.)
 Includes bibliographical references and index.
 ISBN 978-1-61913-383-9 (hard cover : alk. paper)
 1. New York (State)--Juvenile literature. I. Title.
 F119.3.R63 2012
 974.7--dc23
                          2012015608

Printed in the United States of America in North Mankato, Minnesota
1 2 3 4 5 6 7 8 9 16 15 14 13 12

052012
WEP040512

Project Coordinator: Karen Durrie
Art Director: Terry Paulhus

Weigl acknowledges Getty Images as the primary image supplier for this title.

NEW YORK

Contents

2 AV² Book Code

4 Nickname

6 Location

8 History

10 Flower and Seal

12 Flag

14 Animal

16 Capital

18 Goods

20 Fun Things to Do

22 Facts

24 Key Words

This is New York. It is called the Empire State.

New York got its nickname from George Washington.

This is the shape of New York. It is in the east part of the United States. New York is next to the Atlantic Ocean.

Where is New York?

Canada

N
W E
S

Pacific Ocean

United States

Atlantic Ocean

Mexico

New York borders Canada and five other states.

New York had many early settlers. Dutch settlers came to the area in the 1600s. They made a town called New Amsterdam.

British settlers later changed the name from New Amsterdam to New York.

The rose is the state flower of New York. Roses can be many different colors.

The New York state seal has an American eagle, a globe, and a shield.

The shield shows ships on a river, a grassy shore, mountains, and a large Sun.

This is the state flag of New York. Part of the state seal is in the middle of the flag.

The two women on the flag stand for liberty and justice.

13

The state animal of New York is the beaver. The beaver makes its home close to rivers and streams.

Beavers use rocks and mud to build their homes.

The capital city of New York is Albany. Albany sits on the Hudson River.

Albany has been the state capital since 1797.

New York is home to many factories. There are 18,000 factories in New York. These factories make things such as shoes, cameras, and cookies.

Many newspapers, books, movies, and TV shows are made in New York City.

People from all over the world come to visit New York. They like the bright lights of the big city.

The beautiful mountains, lakes, and rivers also bring many people to New York.

NEW YORK FACTS

These pages provide detailed information that expands on the interesting facts found in the book. These pages are intended to be used by adults as a learning support to help young readers round out their knowledge of each state in the *Explore the U.S.A.* series.

Pages 4–5

New York's nickname, the Empire State, is thought to have come from President George Washington. In 1784, he called New York the "seat of empire." This is likely a reference to New York's wealth and resources. Today, New York leads the country in manufacturing, finance, education, and the arts.

Pages 6–7

On July 26, 1788, New York joined the United States as its 11th state. New York borders New Jersey and Pennsylvania to the south and the New England states of Connecticut, Massachusetts, and Vermont to the east. The Canadian provinces of Ontario and Quebec border New York to the north and west. The south shore of New York's Long Island is on the Atlantic Ocean.

Pages 8–9

The Algonquian Indians have lived in the Hudson Valley and Long Island areas for centuries. When the Dutch arrived, they established the first European settlement near Albany. New York signed the Declaration of Independence in 1776. In 1789, President George Washington lived in New York City, which was the first United States capital.

Pages 10–11

The rose grows naturally throughout North America. The mountains, river, and meadows on the state seal symbolize the diverse landscapes of New York. The ships symbolize the importance of national and foreign commerce. The eagle stands for the United States. It protects the globe, which represents bringing together the old and the new.

Pages 12–13

The ladies Liberty and Justice hold the shield. Liberty's left foot stands on a crown, symbolizing New York's freedom from Great Britain. Justice is blindfolded and holds a sword in one hand and a scale in the other. This represents fairness in the law. The bottom of the seal has New York's state motto, *Excelsior*. This is Latin for "Ever Upward."

Pages 14–15

The beaver became the state animal in 1975. Early fur traders settled in what is now Albany to trade beaver pelts with American Indians. Beavers are known as nature's engineers because they change the landscape to create ponds for their homes. They carry rocks and mud with their front paws and wood between their teeth.

Pages 16–17

Albany is one of the oldest settlements of the original 13 colonies. It began in 1614 when a fort was built on the site where the city now stands. Albany covers 21 square miles (54 square kilometers) and has a population of about 94,000 people. It is located about 150 miles (240 kilometers) north of New York City.

Pages 18–19

New York factories produce electrical, medical, and computer equipment. They also make clothing, plastics, and chemicals. Millions of people all over the world read *The New York Times*. Wall Street is home to many of the world's largest banks. The New York Stock Exchange is a driving force in the nation's economy.

Pages 20–21

Visitors are attracted to the varied activities available in New York. Many visit the theaters, restaurants, and attractions in New York City. Niagara Falls, a world-renowned tourist destination, lies between New York and Canada. Tourists also enjoy the beautiful wilderness of the Adirondack Mountains and the beaches of Long Island.

KEY WORDS

Research has shown that as much as 65 percent of all written material published in English is made up of 300 words. These 300 words cannot be taught using pictures or learned by sounding them out. They must be recognized by sight. This book contains 64 common sight words to help young readers improve their reading fluency and comprehension. This book also teaches young readers several important content words, such as proper nouns. These words are paired with pictures to aid in learning and improve understanding.

Page	Sight Words First Appearance
4	from, got, is, it, its, state, the, this
7	and, in, next, of, other, part, to, where
8	a, came, changed, had, in, later, made, many, name, they
11	American, an, be, can, different, has, large, mountains, on, river, shows
12	for, two
15	animal, close, home, makes, their, use
16	been, city
19	as, are, books, such, that, there, these, things
21	all, also, big, come, lights, like, over, people, world

Page	Content Words First Appearance
4	George Washington, New York, nickname
7	Atlantic Ocean, Canada, shape, United States
8	area, New Amsterdam, settlers, town
11	colors, eagle, flower, globe, rose, seal, shield, ships, shore, Sun
12	flag, justice, liberty, middle, women
15	beaver, streams, tails
16	Albany, capital, Hudson River
19	cameras, cookies, factories, movies, New York City, newspapers, shoes, TV shows
21	lakes

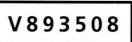